NATURE WE NEED

Why Do We Need POOP?

by Laura K. Murray

PEBBLE
a capstone imprint

Published by Pebble, an imprint of Capstone
1710 Roe Crest Drive, North Mankato, Minnesota 56003
capstonepub.com

Library of Congress Cataloging-in-Publication Data is available on the Library of Congress website.

ISBN: 9780756575359 (hardcover)
ISBN: 9780756575304 (paperback)
ISBN: 9780756575311 (ebook PDF)

Summary: Ever ask yourself, "Do we really need poop?" Well, the answer is...YES! In this Pebble Explore book, discover how this not-so-lovely part of nature is essential to our world. In fact, we need poop to help crops grow and replenish soil. Certain animals even eat poop for nutrients!

Editorial Credits
Editor: Donald Lemke; Designer: Sarah Bennett; Media Researcher: Svetlana Zhurkin; Production Specialist: Katy LaVigne

Image Credits
Dreamstime: Clara Cabezas, 20; Getty Images: alexei_tm, 25, Cloebudgie, 29 (bottom), fdevalera, 17, Gallo Images, 13, GregorBister, 16, izanbar, 9, JossK, 10, LA Waterhouse Photography, 21, mscornelius, 4, Whiteway, 29 (middle); Shutterstock: Alen Thien, 11, Alexey Morozov, 19, Clara Bastian, cover, David Calvert, 18, Faith Forrest (dotted background), cover and throughout, Francisco Martinez Lanzas, 12, hamdi bendali, 27, JamesChen, 14, Jeffrey B. Banke, 29 (top), jennyt, 24, kram-9, 28, Lens Quest, 7, Lorraine Logan, 5, Marco Tomasini, 8, Photo Fun, 6, Pixelheld, 8 (inset), pumab, 23, Reinhold Leitner (brown texture), cover, back cover, and throughout, Vladimir Wrangel, 15

Printed and bound in the USA. 5425

Table of Contents

Words in **bold** are in the glossary.

Leaving Clues

A black bear and her cub are close by. They left tracks in the forest. They also left piles of fresh poop. The poop contains seeds and bones. The bears have been eating berries and fish. Bear poop spreads seeds across the forest. The seeds will grow into new plants.

Everything that eats also poops. Poop has important jobs in **nature**. It helps plants grow. It gives humans clues about wildlife. Animals use poop in all sorts of ways.

All About Poop

Poop is solid waste. It's what is left of food that animals did not **digest**. Animal poop can contain hair, bones, scales, berries, seeds, and bug parts.

earthworm

earthworm castings

An animal's body breaks down food. This helps the animal get energy and **nutrients** from the food. The rest passes out of its body.

Poop has many names. It may be called scat, droppings, or dung. Bat poop is called **guano**. Caterpillar poop is known as frass. Earthworm droppings are castings.

Animal poop can be hard or soft. It can be smooth or lumpy. Poop has different smells too.

Some animal poop is shaped like a tube. Deer and rabbits poop small balls called pellets. Wombats poop in cubes!

wombat

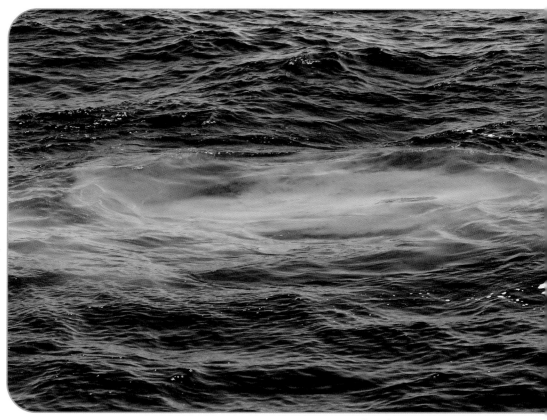

whale poop

Poop can be brown, black, green, yellow, or other colors. An animal's diet changes the color of its poop. Whales eat lots of shrimp-like animals. This diet makes their poop pink, orange, or red.

Animals use their poop in many ways. It helps them send messages to other animals. Some bury their poop. Others leave it in place. They use it as a warning to stay away.

Hippos mark their area with poop. They spin their tail. They spray clouds of poop underwater.

bird-dropping spider

Poop can keep animals safe. The bird-dropping spider looks like white poop from a bird. Other animals do not want to eat these spiders.

Some animals feed on poop.
Egyptian vultures eat yellow cow dung.
The dung has nutrients. It makes the
birds' beaks bright yellow. A brightly
colored beak helps them find a mate.

Dung beetles feed on poop from cows, elephants, and other animals. They roll dung into a ball and bury it. A dung beetle can bury dung that is 250 times heavier than itself!

Female dung beetles lay their eggs inside the balls. The poop is food for the babies. It keeps them safe too.

How Does Poop Help Us?

Animals spread nutrients and seeds in their poop. Birds, bats, and other animals eat fruit from plants and trees. The seeds come out in their droppings. They grow into new plants and trees.

tambaqui fish

Fish poop helps rivers, lakes, and oceans. Tambaqui fish eat fruit and plant seeds. Their poop moves through the water. Then the seeds can grow into new plants in other places.

Humans study poop to learn more about animals. Scat gives clues about what animals are in the area. Poop can show if an animal is healthy or sick.

dinosaur dung fossil

Scientists study poop from millions of years ago. The poop helps them learn lots of information. People look at the size and shape of poop. They study poop through a microscope. The poop can show what food the animal ate.

Farmers and gardeners use animal poop as **fertilizer**. It is called manure. Manure adds nutrients to the soil. It can help plants and crops grow.

People may **compost** manure for a time. This breaks down the manure. It helps kill germs. It doesn't smell as bad either. Sometimes people make manure into dry pellets. Other times they grow worms on the manure. Worm poop is rich in nutrients.

Humans use animal poop in many ways. People use livestock manure for fuel. The manure is made into gases and liquids. It gets turned into heat and electricity. People use **fibers** from animal poop to make paper and building materials.

Some people use dried poop to make fires.

llama poop

Poop can even be used to clean. Scientists use llama poop to clean dirty water. Helpful **bacteria** in the poop take out pollutants in the water.

Threats to Poop

All parts of nature are linked. They need each other. Today plants and animals have many threats.

The number of animals is dropping. People are taking over the places animals live. **Climate change** is another threat to wildlife. There are fewer animals spreading seeds. It makes it harder for plants to grow.

Humans must be careful around animal poop. It carries germs. It can cause disease.

Raccoons and other animals may carry tiny roundworms. The eggs come out in the animals' poop. One dropping can have more than 10 million eggs!

Poop from cats, dogs, and other pets can cause sickness too. People need to clean up after their pets. They should not feed or touch wild animals. They should wash their hands after being outside.

A World Without Poop

Can you imagine a world without poop? Animals would not be able to get rid of their waste. They would not survive. The soil would be less healthy. Many plants and trees would not be able to grow. They would disappear. Food would be harder to find.

Animals would have to change how they live. They could not use poop for warnings or other messages. Dung beetles would not be able to eat or raise their young.

Every animal is different. So is their poop! Poop is an important part of nature. Humans, plants, and animals need poop.

COOL FACTS ABOUT POOP

- Female wild turkeys poop in a spiral shape. Males poop in the shape of the letter "J."

- Some snakes may not poop for more than 400 days.

- Rabbits poop about 500 pellets a day. This would be like a human pooping once every three minutes.

- Vultures poop on their own legs to stay cool and kill germs.

- Sloths climb down from their tree about once a week to poop. They wiggle or dance before climbing back up.

- Otter dung (called spraint) can smell like violets.

Glossary

bacteria (bak-TEER-ee-uh)—very small living things that exist everywhere in nature

climate change (KLY-muht CHAYNJ)—a significant change in Earth's climate over a period of time

compost (KOM-pohst)—mixture of decaying leaves, vegetables, and other items that make the soil better for farming and gardening

digest (dy-GEST)—to break down food so it can be used by the body

fertilizer (FUHR-tuh-ly-zuhr)—a substance used to make crops grow better

fibers (FY-buhrz)—threads found in vegetables and other materials

guano (GWAH-noh)—a type of bird or bat dropping that is often rich in nutrients

nature (NAY-chuhr)—the world around us, including all of the plants, animals, and other living things

nutrient (NOO-tree-uhnt)—a substance needed by a living thing to stay healthy

Read More

Curtis, Jennifer Keats and Julianne Ubigau. *Pooper Snooper*. Mt. Pleasant, SC: Arbordale Publishing, 2021.

Furstinger, Nancy. *How Do Sloths Poop?* North Mankato, MN: Capstone, 2019.

Lundgren, Julie K. *Things That Poop in the Night!* New York: Crabtree, 2023.

Internet Sites

BioKIDS, University of Michigan: Scat and Pellets
biokids.umich.edu/guides/tracks_and_sign/leavebehind/scat/

Internet Center for Wildlife Damage Management: Scat ID
icwdm.org/identification/feces/scat-id/

Scout Life: Can You Identify This Animal Poop?
scoutlife.org/quizzes/153553/can-you-identify-this-animal-poop/

Index

About the Author

Laura K. Murray is a Minnesota-based author of more than 100 published or forthcoming books for young readers. She loves learning from fellow readers and helping others find their reading superpowers!
Visit her at LauraKMurray.com.